PROTECTING ENDANGERED SPECIES AT THE SAN DIEGO ZOO

ZOO WORLD

PROTECTING ENDANGERED SPECIES AT THE SAN DIEGO ZOO

BY GEORGEANNE IRVINE

SCHOLASTIC INC.
New York Toronto London Auckland Sydney

To my beloved mother, "Mommy Dot," who let the little girl in the red cowboy hat sleep with dozens of stuffed toy animals surrounding her every night, and who taught her appreciation, love and concern for living creatures of all kinds.

ACKNOWLEDGMENTS

Thank you to my friends and colleagues—Kathy Marmack, Heidi Ensley, Carlee Robinson, Helena Fitch-Snyder, Don Lindburg, Craig Racicot, Ron Garrison, Randy Reiches, Sharon Joseph, Cyndi Kuehler, Kim Livingstone, Art Risser, Susan Schafer, Oliver Ryder, Jeff Jouett, Michael McKeever, Victoria Garrison and Karen Hickey. Without your help and inspiration, this book would never have come into being.

PHOTO CREDITS

Ron Garrison: front cover, endsheets; 6 top left and right, lower left; 10; 11 lower left and right; 12; 13; 14; 15; 16; 17; 18 left; 19 left and lower; 20 top; 21; 22; 23; 24 lower; 25; 26; 27; 30; 31; 32; 33; 34; 39 lower; 41 lower; 42; 43 left. Heidi Ensley: 5; 18 right; 19 top right; 20 lower. Helena Fitch-Snyder: 6 lower right; 35; 36 lower; 37; 38; 39 top. Carol Ann Gallagher: 36 top. Craig MacFarland: 24 top. Craig Racicot: 9; 11 top; 28; 40; 41 top; 43 right. Randy Reiches: 29.

 Published by Scholastic Inc.,
730 Broadway, New York, NY 10003,
by arrangement with Simon & Schuster, Inc.
Designed by Kathleen Westray.
Printed in the U.S.A.
ISBN 0-590-46864-2
2 3 4 5 6 7 8 9 10 08 99 98 97 96 95 94 93 92

CONTENTS

INTRODUCTION

THE YEAR WAS 1810. The farmers, families, and townsfolk of a small Kentucky community just couldn't wait for the passenger pigeon flock to arrive. Millions upon millions of the cooing pigeons were coming to nest in the nearby forest.

The people gathered their guns, cooking pots, hungry hogs and hounds, and headed for the edge of the forest. Passenger pigeons meant a tasty feast for everybody!

Before anyone even caught a glimpse of the attractive blue-and-chestnut-colored pigeons, they heard them. The wingbeats and calls of so many birds made it sound like Thor, the mythical god of thunder, was waging a war against silence.

As the passenger pigeons arrived overhead, the sky darkened. There were so many birds, they blocked out the sunlight. As soon as the beautiful birds began to roost in the trees, the people began to shoot.

"Don't worry, son," a man said to a freckle-faced boy beside him. "There are billions of these birds in the world. It won't hurt to kill a few."

Indo-Chinese leopard

Bornean orangutan

And billions of passenger pigeons there were... yet at 1 P.M. on September 1, 1914, Martha, the very last passenger pigeon on earth, died at the Cincinnati Zoo. She was twenty-nine years old. The passenger pigeon species had become extinct! The billions of birds were gone forever because of drastic overhunting by humans.

Years earlier, on August 12, 1883, a zebralike animal called a quagga died at the Amsterdam Zoo in Europe. She was the last of her species in the world. All of the other quaggas had been killed by hunters as the animals roamed in herds across the plains of southern Africa.

And in the late 1600s, the last dodo birds

Giant panda

Martha, the last passenger pigeon

Przewalski's wild horses

Cheetah

Grevy's zebra

Lowland gorilla

vanished from their island home of Mauritius in the Indian Ocean. Dutch settlers had clubbed and shot every last one of these chubby, flightless birds that waddled as they walked.

In the world today, many other animals face extinction. These animals that were once very common and are now very rare are called endangered species. Giant pandas, orangutans, tigers, gorillas, bald eagles, and elephants are all endangered species. It's hard to imagine a world without them, but there are now so few of these animals left that they really may become extinct unless something is done to save them.

Bald eagle

African elephants

Sumatran tiger

Animals are dying because they are losing their natural habitats. Rain forests are being cut down; swamps are being drained; cities are replacing grasslands. The animals literally have nowhere to go.

Poachers, too, kill many exotic animals. A poacher is a hunter who kills a rare animal even though it is against the law. Beautiful big cats like leopards, jaguars, and tigers are hunted for their fur. Elephants are killed so people can make jewelry out of their ivory tusks, and rhinoceroses die so people can have their horns, which some think have magical powers.

Although the future looks dim for many species, there is hope for others. Zoos are playing an important role in helping governments and conservation groups save animals from extinction.

The San Diego Zoo and the San Diego Wild Animal Park are two of the finest zoos in the world, and both are well-known for their endangered species conservation efforts. A special part of the Zoo and the Wild Animal Park is the Center for Reproduction of Endangered Species, called CRES for short. CRES scientists are working on many projects that will protect and conserve endangered animals.

Cheetahs, Grévy's zebras, Arabian oryx, Sumatran tigers, lowland gorillas, ruffed lemurs, white rhinoceroses, Fiji Island iguanas, red crowned cranes, California condors, golden conures, sloth bears, Przewalski's wild horses, Malayan tapirs, slender-horned gazelles, and douc langur monkeys are only a few members of endangered species that have been born at the San Diego Zoo and the San Diego Wild Animal Park. Each year, the list grows longer because of the caring, concerned, and dedicated people who work there.

For every rare animal birth, there's an interesting tale to tell. What follow are stories about some very special animals. Each species is endangered, but hopes are high that these creatures will never become extinct like the unfortunate dodos, quaggas, and passenger pigeons.

Fiji Island iguanas

Golden conure

ASIA AND HER CUBS

CLOUDED LEOPARD CUBS were due to be born any day at the San Diego Zoo, and Asia, the mother-to-be, wanted another butterfish. Since she'd become pregnant, two-year-old Asia was always hungry. Even after she had finished a big bowl of food, Asia would whine for more of the silvery, savory butterfish.

Asia was a star in the Zoo's Animal Chit-Chat Show. She had been hand-raised by humans, so she was friendly enough for animal trainers to handle her. Asia's two clouded leopard friends, Dahan and Rimau, were hand-raised by humans, too. Asia and the males got along fine because they had met when they were young. Their friendship was quite unusual, since adult male clouded leopards normally fight with the females.

Asia has a meal of butterfish.

Dahan leaping

Each day in the Animal Chit-Chat Show, when Asia or the males leaped on stage with trainer Kathy or Heidi, people learned that clouded leopards are one of the rarest wild cats in the world. They are an endangered species from the rain forests of Southeast Asia. Because they have such big fangs, some people think clouded leopards are distant relatives of the saber-toothed tiger, a big cat that became extinct thousands of years ago.

Now Asia was taking a four-month break from the show to have cubs, and Dahan was the father. Asia's trainers were very excited because clouded leopard cubs are seldom born in zoos. They were a little worried, too. The trainers were concerned that Asia might not know how to care for her cubs because she had been hand-raised.

Ten days before Asia's cubs were due to be born, the trainers put a large nest box filled with straw in her pen. A video camera was attached to the ceiling of the box. The trainers would now be able to watch Asia have her babies on a nearby video monitor, and they'd be able to see if Asia was caring for them.

A round-the-clock clouded leopard birth watch began. Kathy and the other trainers took turns spending the night at the Zoo with their eyes glued to Asia's video monitor. Sometimes, the soon-to-be mom cried for attention. When a

Dahan, Rimau and Asia with a black leopard, a cheetah, and their trainers

trainer would sit in the pen with Asia for a short time, Asia would plop herself in the trainer's lap so her human friend could pet her.

One cold March night, a few minutes before midnight, trainer Carlee had just settled in for an evening of clouded leopard video-viewing. Asia, who was usually asleep at this time, was extremely restless. She tossed and turned in her nest box. Although it was dark, Carlee could tell that Asia was having a baby.

Asia stays close to baby Pu-ying.

Straw makes a comfortable nest for Pu-ying.

Carlee wanted to shout and jump for joy, but instead she remained very quiet. She didn't want to disturb the new mother leopard as she licked her cub clean. Soon, Asia became restless again. Carlee watched as another cub was born, and as Asia cleaned this baby, too.

The next morning, Asia let the Zoo veterinarian look at her cubs to make sure they were healthy. Both cubs were nursing from their mother! Carlee, Kathy, Heidi, and another trainer, Amy, were as excited as could be. Never in the history of the San Diego Zoo had a clouded leopard mom ever cared for her own cubs.

The cubs were tiny, each weighing only a little more than a stick of butter. Their eyes were still closed, and their fur was quite dark. One cub was a female and the other, a male. They were named Pu-ying and Pu-chai, after Thai words that mean "female" and "male."

Pu-ying and Pu-chai grew quickly, opening their eyes when they were thirteen days old. When they were three weeks old, they crept out of the nest box and into the warm sunshine for the very first time.

To everyone's surprise, Asia was the perfect mother. She always kept an eye on her babies in

Pu-chai sneaks out of the nest box.

Leopard cubs are good at getting into mischief.

case they got into mischief. If Pu-ying whimpered because she climbed to the roof of the nest box and couldn't get down, Asia rushed to the rescue. She showed her cubs how to jump from the nest box roof to a nearby platform and then to the ground.

Soon Pu-ying and her brother, Pu-chai, were climbing and jumping on and off everything in their pen. Trainer Heidi dangled an old tire on a rope from the top of their cage. The cubs loved to leap from the nest box roof onto the tire. Back and forth they would swing. The frisky cubs were daring, diving clouded leopard acrobats!

Pu-chai with trainer Kathy

Trainer Amy weighs Pu-chai.

Seven-month-old Pu-ying and Pu-chai

Caring for the cubs was a full-time job for Asia. Often, while the cubs napped in the nest box, Asia would sneak away for a quiet time by herself. Sometimes she wanted her trainers to come into the pen to give her extra attention; but the minute Asia heard Pu-ying and Pu-chai stirring, she hurried to check on them.

Every week, the trainers weighed Pu-ying and Pu-chai. Trainer Amy carried the scale right into the clouded leopards' pen. The cubs whimpered a little when Amy picked them up, but they let Amy weigh them, anyway.

One morning, when Pu-ying and Pu-chai were seven months old, Kathy told the other trainers that the cubs would be leaving soon. Since they were almost grown up, they must go to another zoo. There, each cub would meet a new clouded leopard mate.

Although it was hard to say good-bye to young Pu-ying and Pu-chai, Kathy, Carlee, Heidi, and Amy felt happy. They knew that the cubs' birth was an important step toward saving the endangered clouded leopard species from extinction. And they hoped that someday, Pu-ying and Pu-chai would become parents to their own cubs. Now, too, the trainers were certain that Asia would be a good mother to all the cubs she would have in the future.

TORTOISE NUMBER 21 GOES HOME

TORTOISE NUMBER 21 was different from all of the other Galápagos tortoises at the San Diego Zoo. He never wanted to be with the other giant tortoises. When the others huddled together in their barn at night, Number 21 slept in a corner by himself. While the rest of the tortoise herd napped in the shade or lounged in the sun during the day, Number 21 explored the pen.

He was much more alert than the other giant tortoises, and more curious, too. Number 21 liked to stretch his long neck way up high so he could have a better view all around him. By reaching his head high, Number 21 was also showing that he was a dominant tortoise. In Galápagos tortoise language, the higher an animal can reach with its head, the more dominant that tortoise is.

Tortoise 21 has a saddle-shaped shell.

The Zoo's other tortoises are bigger than Number 21.

Tortoise Number 21 even looked different from his tortoise neighbors. He was one of the smallest of the adult Galápagos tortoises, and his shell was unusual, too. It looked like it had been pulled up in front, like the brim of a hat that has been bent back. His entire shell actually resembled a saddle.

All of the Zoo's giant tortoises had come from the Galápagos Islands. This group of small islands is located in the Pacific Ocean about 600 miles off the coast of Ecuador, a country in South America.

At one time, tens of thousands of the huge land turtles lived on the many Galápagos Islands. Some of them were probably over a hundred years old. Tortoises native to the various islands looked and acted different from each other. In the 1600s, sailors began stopping at the Galápagos Islands. The sailors filled their ships' holds with Galápagos tortoises so they could eat fresh tortoise meat during their long sea voyages. They also introduced goats, dogs, cats, rats, and other animals to the islands. These new animals devoured the plants that were food for the giant tortoises, and sometimes killed the baby tortoises.

It wasn't long before very few Galápagos tortoises were left in their native homeland. They had become an endangered species.

In 1960, the Charles Darwin Research Center was built on one of the Galápagos Islands. A goal of the Center was to save the giant tortoises, as well as other wildlife and plants from extinction. The San Diego Zoo sent money to help fund some of the work. In addition, the Zoo was attempting to raise Galápagos tortoises in San Diego.

The director of the Charles Darwin Research Center visited the San Diego Zoo in 1976. While inspecting the tortoises, he discovered that Number 21 was a rare Galápagos tortoise from Hood Island. The Hood Island tortoises were known by their saddle-shaped shells and smaller size.

A Galápagos Island sunset

Most of Hood Island's giant tortoises had died because goats ate all their food. Only two males and twelve females were left on the island! Because Hood Island is big, scientists worried that the remaining tortoises wouldn't find each other to mate. So all of the Hood Island tortoises were taken to the Charles Darwin Research Center. There, the adults could be together and, it was hoped, baby tortoises would soon be hatching from their eggs.

Since there were only two other male Hood

Galápagos tortoise hatching

Scientists release Tortoise 21.

Number 21 is the father of over 170 babies.

Island tortoises, the San Diego Zoo agreed to send Number 21 back to the Charles Darwin Research Center. The 200-pound land turtle traveled by jet to Equador in a sturdy, padded crate. From there, a cruise ship named the *Iguana* sailed to the Galápagos Islands with Number 21 on board. At the Research Center, Number 21 joined the other Hood Island tortoises, who looked just like him.

A few years later, exciting news reached the San Diego Zoo. Number 21 was the father of three baby tortoises! The tortoise who liked to be alone in San Diego was at last with his own kind and, by 1988, had fathered over 170 young tortoises... many more than either of the other two Hood Island males.

Other exciting news was that all of the plant-eating goats had been removed from Hood Island. With the goats gone, the plants that the tortoises needed for food grew back, and some of Number 21's offspring were returned to their native Hood Island home. Once again the giant tortoises could survive there because they now had food.

Number 21 is a very special Galápagos tortoise because he is playing a major role in saving the tortoises with the saddle-shaped shells from becoming extinct. And he's not such a different tortoise after all...not when he is with other Hood Island tortoises.

JUDY, A BLOCK WALL, AND A BABY RHINO

JUDY IS A RARE black rhinoceros who has a very unusual habit. She likes to stand next to cement block walls!

When Judy first came to the San Diego Wild Animal Park in late 1986 from Chicago's Brookfield Zoo, keeper Randy wondered if she'd ever have a baby. Judy was already twenty years old and had never given birth before.

Although Judy was born in the wilds of Africa, she had spent most of her life at the Brookfield Zoo. At the zoo, she lived in a cement block pen with a male and another female black rhinoceros.

The other female didn't like Judy at all. She pushed Judy around and chased her. Every time the male black rhino tried to be friendly with Judy, the other female kept Judy away from him.

Judy next to a cement block wall

Cornelius

When Judy was scared or nervous, she stood against the back wall of her pen, as far from the dominant female as possible. Judy felt safe by the cement block wall. It was like a security blanket.

Because black rhinos are an endangered species, Judy was sent to the Wild Animal Park in hopes that she would have a baby there. She was to be a mate for the Park's male black rhino, Cornelius, in the East Africa enclosure.

Judy's new East Africa home was a wide, open area as big as some entire zoos. She'd have plenty of room to roam and to share with the giraffes, antelopes, Cape buffalos, and other rhinos that also live in this new East Africa habitat.

During her first thirty days at the Park, Judy lived alone in a pen called a boma in the middle of the East Africa habitat. Veterinarians and keepers watched Judy to make sure she was healthy. The walls of the boma were made of cement blocks, so Judy felt comfortable and safe there.

The day Judy was released from the boma, she was nervous because she wasn't used to being around so many different animals. She chased the giraffes to keep them out of her way. She charged at the keepers' trucks as they drove by with food for the animals. She spent much of her time where she felt the safest...right next to the cement block wall of the boma.

Slowly, Judy explored her new home; and before long, she got used to the other animals and the keepers' trucks. She also became friendly with Cornelius, the male black rhinoceros. She even discovered a few other cement block walls in the habitat besides those of the boma.

Within six months of Judy's arrival at the Wild Animal Park, she ate at animal feeders, standing next to antelopes and Cape buffalos. She nibbled carrots and leaves fed to her by keepers from the backs of their trucks. But best of all, Judy the black rhinoceros was expecting a baby! Cornelius was going to be a father.

The thought of Judy having a baby made Randy and the other keepers happy. Her new Wild Animal Park home had made a difference.

Judy's baby and every other black rhinoceros birth is valuable and important. Many black rhinos are dying in their native Africa. Since 1970, poachers have killed most of Africa's 65,000 black rhinoceroses for their horns. Now, only 3,500 are left in Africa and less than 200 in zoos.

Keeper Sharon feeds Judy leafy plants and carrots.

Jioni was born in a block wall boma.

Jioni gulps gallons of milk daily.

Some day, Jioni will have a horn like his mother's.

Just before Judy's baby was due, the keepers moved her back into the block wall boma. If Judy had a problem delivering her baby, the veterinarian could easily help her, and Judy still liked the security of the cement block wall.

Judy didn't need any help from the veterinarian, however. One sunny September morning, when keepers Randy, Sharon, and Mike got to work, Judy greeted them with a healthy male rhino calf by her side. Newborn Jioni was only hours old, and very cute.

Jioni was small for a black rhinoceros calf. He

Judy charges at Cornelius.

was barely tall enough to nurse from his mother, and had to stretch his short rhino body to reach Judy's nipple. The keepers smiled because Jioni reminded them of a little dog. He looked like a playful puppy as he galloped around the boma, exploring every inch of it.

Since Jioni was an unusually small rhino calf, he and Judy stayed in the boma by themselves for several weeks. Before he could go out among the other animals, Jioni had to grow.

Like most rhino calves, Jioni was a big eater. He gulped down almost three gallons of his mother's rich, sweet milk each day. In a month, Jioni gained ninety pounds and was ready to leave the boma with his mother.

As the boma gate was opened by the keepers, baby Jioni poked his head outside for a first glimpse of other animals. He trotted into the East Africa habitat with Judy close behind. Within minutes, Jioni's father, Cornelius, approached the baby rhino to look at him. Because Judy was a protective mother, she charged between Cornelius and her calf. Poor curious Cornelius was chased away by Judy.

Judy never let Jioni out of her sight. As time passed, though, the new rhino mom became more relaxed. She even allowed Cornelius near the baby when Jioni was six months old. Cornelius was a calm, patient rhinoceros father who played with his son. He even let frisky Jioni charge at him.

Each day now, as Wild Animal Park keepers drive around the East Africa habitat caring for the animals, they look for Judy and Jioni. Sometimes, they see the mother rhino and calf sharing a feeder with antelopes or Cape buffalos. At other times, the pair is seen walking past giraffes or sitting with Cornelius. But if Judy and Jioni are nowhere else in sight in the big, open East Africa enclosure, the keepers know just where to find them. They are resting peacefully together by Judy's comfortable security spot...a cement block wall!

In the East Africa habitat, Jioni and Judy roam among other animals.

Jioni and Judy still like to spend time near block walls.

TOO FEW TAHITIAN LORY CHICKS

BIRDKEEPER KIM was concerned. The rare Tahitian lory female had been sitting on two tiny white eggs for twenty-seven days, and they still hadn't hatched. By now, downy, gray chicks should have been peeping for their mother lory to bring them food. Something was terribly wrong!

Kim had been disappointed earlier in the year when the same female lory sat on two other eggs that didn't hatch. One egg was infertile, which means there was no baby bird developing inside. A chick had been growing in the second egg, but it died a few days before it was to hatch. Kim was worried that these new eggs wouldn't hatch, either.

Kim called zoologist Cyndi to discuss the problem. Cyndi helps manage the San Diego Zoo's Tahitian lory breeding program, so she might know what to do.

Cyndi knew that the precious eggs should have hatched by now. She felt chances were slim that they contained living lory chicks. Usually, lory eggs hatch within twenty-five days. Cyndi and Kim carefully placed the fragile eggs in a warm thermos half filled with birdseed. Then they carried them to the Zoo's Bird Propagation Center. The "Prop Center" is a building where eggs hatch and keepers raise rare baby birds.

At the Prop Center, Cyndi candled the eggs, which means she held them up to a special light in a darkened room. This allowed her to see through the thin eggshell. Cyndi and Kim were very disappointed to find out that one of the eggs was infertile, and the second contained a chick who had died a few days earlier...just like the other two eggs!

Hatching and raising Tahitian lory chicks has been a problem ever since these violet-blue parrots with the bright orange beaks and white bibs arrived in San Diego in 1978. U.S. Customs agents had given eight rare Tahitian lories to the Zoo after they took them from smugglers who had tried to sneak the birds into the country.

Although a few Tahitian lories have hatched and survived at the Zoo over the years, the hopes had been for hundreds by now. Cyndi's job is to find out what is wrong. This is no easy task because very little is known about Tahitian lories. Cyndi can't ask bird experts from other zoos because no other zoos have these birds. And the few private bird breeders who own Tahitian lories don't know any more than Cyndi.

What *is* known about these tiny parrots is that

Keeper Kim feeds papaya to the lories.

Tahitian lories are comical parrots.

Tahitian lories are so rare, they are an endangered species. They come from remote, isolated islands in French Polynesia, and are already extinct on the bigger, more populated islands like Tahiti and Bora Bora. Bird experts have never even studied the habits of these comical, curious lories in the wild.

Tahitian lories are rare for many reasons. Some have been killed by severe tropical storms, others by harrier hawks and rats that were brought to the islands by humans. Still other Tahitian lories have died from malaria, a terrible disease carried by mosquitoes that were accidently brought to the islands on aircraft. Lories captured by smugglers for the pet trade have died, too, because people don't know how to care for the birds properly. Finally, the forests where the Tahitian lories live and nest are being destroyed for lumber and to create farmland.

To raise any birds successfully in captivity, keepers must understand the birds' behavior and habits. They must know the exact types and quantities of foods they eat, the kinds of nesting materials they use, and the illnesses they may acquire.

In San Diego, Cyndi and other Zoo bird experts have learned a few things about Tahitian lories, but not enough to save the species from extinction—at least, not yet. Right now, there are more questions about the blue-violet birds than answers.

They have learned that a Tahitian lory may be friendly to its mate one minute, and very mean and aggressive to it the next minute. The lories may also break their eggs or hurt their babies. To prevent this, all Tahitian lory eggs are incubated

Zoologist Cyndi examines a lory egg.

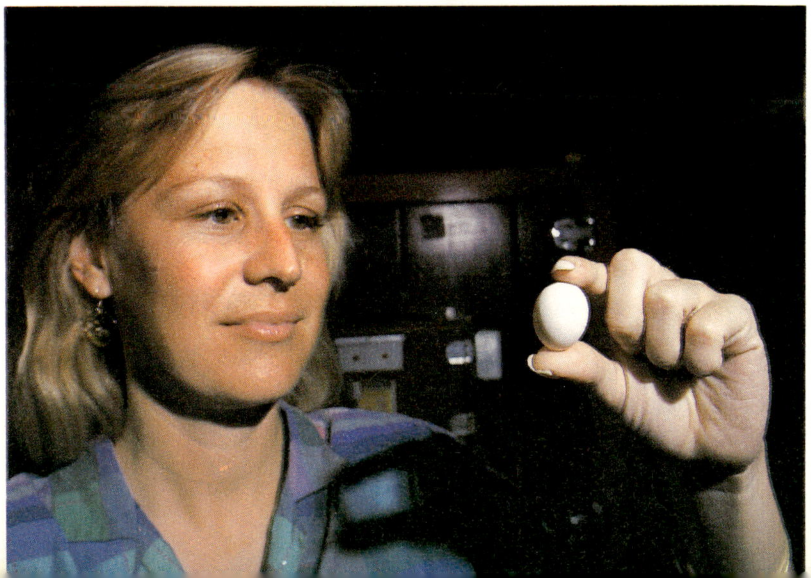

Newly-hatched lory

Tahitian lories could become extinct soon.

at the Prop Center, away from the parents. If the eggs do hatch, Cyndi and the keepers know how to hand-raise the babies. They are very tiny and must be fed every hour.

Keeping the Tahitian lories alive once they're adults is even more difficult. Cyndi knows they eat pollen, nectar, flowers, and bugs... but how much and exactly what types is still a question.

Some female lories lay eggs, but others do not ... and Cyndi still doesn't know why. Some lories die from bacterial infections, but Cyndi and the keepers have trouble preventing these infections.

Although the violet-blue birds with the bright orange beaks and white bibs could become extinct someday soon, Cyndi and other San Diego Zoo bird experts are doing everything they can to prevent this from happening. Cyndi's next step is a visit to French Polynesia to try to gather more Tahitian lory information. She is also writing to bird experts all over the world for their advice.

It's hoped that a Tahitian lory conservation program will be set up between the San Diego Zoo and the French Polynesian government. In the meantime, keepers in San Diego will continue trying to hatch and raise Tahitian lory chicks.

It would be a shame for so beautiful a bird to vanish from the face of the earth, and it would be senseless not to try to save it.

A NEW MONKEY MOM FOR FAROUK

POOR PINT-SIZE FAROUK! He was the newest lion-tailed macaque at the San Diego Zoo, yet he was already an orphan. Shoba, Farouk's natural mother, died when he was only a week old. This made animal behaviorists Don and Helena very sad. Although Farouk was now being cared for by humans in the Zoo nursery, Don and Helena wanted to try a new, special way to raise him.

As behaviorists in the Zoo's Center for Reproduction of Endangered Species, Don and Helena had been studying lion-tailed macaques for many years. By watching them for long periods of time, they were learning much about macaque behavior. This is important because lion-tailed macaques are an endangered monkey species. There are only a few hundred of these acrobatic monkeys in zoos,

Behaviorist Helena with Farouk

Orphaned Farouk meets his new mom.

and less than 2,000 in their rain forest homes in India. Don and Helena's studies were helping the San Diego Zoo put lion-tailed macaques together in family groups so they'd have many babies.

Since baby macaques cuddle and cling to their mothers, Don and Helena decided to raise Farouk with an artificial mother among other lion-tailed macaques. By being around a macaque group, Farouk would learn monkey manners and social skills.

Farouk was three weeks old when he met his artificial mom. Although his new mother didn't look much like a monkey, she was woolly, warm, and huggable—the things that mattered to Farouk. Her body was a wire frame covered with a heating pad and fuzzy fabric. "Mom's" head was simply an opening in the wire where a keeper could fit bottles of milk for Farouk's daily feedings.

Farouk and his new mom lived in a small cage that was placed inside a macaque group's large enclosure each day. Infant Farouk could cling safely to "Mom" while watching older macaque youngsters play monkey chase all day long. The other macaques could slowly get to know Farouk without being able to play roughly with the little guy. At night, Farouk and his woolly, wire mom were moved into the nearby keeper kitchen.

After a few weeks, a small wire tunnel was

added to Farouk's cage so he could scamper out to play with the other young macaques when he wanted to. The tunnel, however, was too small for the other, bigger macaques to climb inside his tiny cage.

Gradually, Farouk spent more and more time out in the big enclosure with the older macaque youngsters. He was two months old now and full of energy. After wild games of monkey chase, the other young macaques scurried back to their monkey moms for cuddling and loving. Instead of clinging to his wire, woolly mom, little Farouk sat by himself on the big cage floor. He hugged his knees while he rocked back and forth.

Farouk's rocking behavior worried Don and Helena. But, fortunately, a few days earlier, they noticed that Sita, an older lion-tailed macaque who lived in the adjacent pen, had begun watching Farouk. Although Sita was now old, she had been a mother to many, many monkey babies. Sita smacked her lips at Farouk. In macaque language, lip-smacking means, "I'm a nice monkey. I want to be your friend." Don and Helena decided to move Farouk away from the other macaques and into Sita's pen. They hoped that Sita would adopt lonely, orphaned Farouk.

Farouk was introduced to Sita as he had been to the other macaques. Farouk, in his small cage, was

A bottle of milk is attached to Farouk's "mom".

Farouk clings to his artificial mom.

Farouk makes friends with Sita.

A keeper feeds Farouk.

put inside Sita's pen. Farouk could climb out but Sita was too big to climb in. Sita was very patient and let Farouk come to her. Within an hour, Farouk was clinging to Sita, who carried him into a nest box for cuddling. Farouk had his real monkey mother!

Farouk didn't need his wire, woolly mom anymore. But he still needed two bottles of milk a day even though he was now old enough to eat fruit, as well. To feed Farouk his milk, a keeper held a bottle up to the wire of Farouk and Sita's cage. The nipple poked through the wire so Farouk could drink. This scared Sita because she worried that her new monkey baby might be taken away from her by the keeper. Sita hit at the bottle and wouldn't let Farouk near it. The keeper bribed Sita with a tasty treat, and Sita learned quickly that if she let Farouk drink his milk, she got a big, ripe banana to eat.

After Farouk and Sita had spent a month and a half together by themselves, the pair was introduced back into Farouk's original macaque group. Farouk was glad to be with the older macaque youngsters again. They raced around the big pen all day long, playing monkey chase. And when the other young macaques cuddled their real monkey moms, Farouk hugged Sita, his own real monkey mom.

Sita quickly adopted Farouk.

18-month-old Farouk

For four years, Farouk lived with his monkey group at the San Diego Zoo. He grew to be a handsome adult with proper monkey manners and amazing acrobatic skills. He could leap through the air farther than the other macaques.

Now, Farouk's home is at another zoo with three lion-tailed macaque females. His new keepers hope he'll be a father soon. And Sita is doing just fine, too. She has already adopted another lion-tailed macaque orphan who needed a real monkey mother to cuddle.

FATIHA, THE MHORR GAZELLE

AS THE MORNING DEW glistened on the grass, San Diego Zoo keeper Craig spotted what he'd been waiting for all morning. A newborn Mhorr gazelle peered out from behind a patch of the dewy grass.

The birth of this fragile female gazelle was extremely important. Her species was already extinct in her homeland, the deserts of northwestern Africa. Hunters had killed the last wild Mhorr gazelle in 1968. Now, the only ones alive anywhere were at the San Diego Zoo, the San Diego Wild Animal Park, and a few other zoos around the world. Any Mhorr gazelle birth was a step toward saving these precious animals from vanishing forever.

Fatiha wobbled to her feet within her first twenty minutes of life. After mother Buffala licked her clean, she wandered away from her infant.

Although Fatiha was hungry, Buffala wouldn't let her baby nurse from her.

For seven hours, keeper Craig watched baby Fatiha and her mother. Buffala still wouldn't care for her baby. Craig thought perhaps Buffala didn't know how to be a good mother.

Because Fatiha had to eat to survive, the only solution was to feed her a milk formula from a bottle. Normally, a baby like Fatiha who is rejected by its mother is taken to the Zoo nursery. There, it is bottle-fed and raised by humans. Sometimes though, when the baby grows up, it's hard to reintroduce it to the other animals. That's because the nursery baby is so used to humans, it doesn't know how to behave around other animals.

Keeper Craig wanted to try something different with Fatiha. He had an unusual idea that had been tried only one other time at the Zoo. Instead of taking Fatiha away from the Mhorr gazelle herd to the nursery, Craig wanted to bottle-feed her in the exhibit.

The nursery workers prepared Fatiha's bottles and brought them to Craig. When Craig fed Fatiha her first bottle, she hungrily slurped it all down in only a few minutes. As Fatiha guzzled her milk, Craig clicked a clicker two or three times. For several days, whenever Craig fed Fatiha, he clicked the clicker a few times.

Fatiha was rejected by her mother, Buffala.

Keeper Craig feeding Fatiha

Craig did not want Fatiha to bond with him.

Fatiha was accepted into the herd.

Fatiha ate five times a day, so she heard a lot of clicking. Within three days, as soon as Fatiha heard Craig's clicker, she knew that food was on the way. Now, Craig simply clicked the clicker as he walked into the Mhorr gazelle exhibit and Fatiha rushed over to receive her bottle.

Craig was careful not to spend too much time with the precious baby. It was important for Fatiha to understand she was a Mhorr gazelle, and to bond with the gazelle herd and not with him.

Fatiha was the first such baby ever to live with the herd. All the others had been rejected by their moms and had been taken to the nursery. Although this new baby was strange to the grown-up Mhorr gazelles, they readily accepted her. Some of the adults even let tiny Fatiha wander through their legs and under their bellies, as if they were bridges.

As Fatiha grew older, she drank fewer bottles of milk each day. When she was three months old, Fatiha no longer needed a bottle. She ate what the big Mhorr gazelles eat—hay and alfalfa pellets. Craig's unusual idea had worked, and Fatiha was a healthy, accepted herd member.

Buffala cared for her next baby.

The following year, another youngster was born to Buffala, Fatiha's mother. Craig was prepared to bottle-feed this baby, too. But he was in for a big surprise. Buffala cared for and nursed her own baby. Craig is not sure, but he thinks it's possible that Buffala learned how to care for her baby by watching Fatiha nurse from the bottle.

The Zoo's Mhorr gazelle herd is continuing to grow. And perhaps someday, if enough Mhorr gazelles are born in zoos, some of them can be returned home to the deserts of northwestern Africa.

WHAT YOU CAN DO FOR ENDANGERED SPECIES

You, too, can become a conservationist and a champion of wildlife. Here are some ways you can help:

1. Recycle aluminum cans, glass, plastic and newspaper. This will help save the tropical rain forests and other animal habitats. Imagine, for every 6-foot-tall stack of newspapers you recycle, one 35-foot-tall tree is spared. And, your television can run for four hours on the energy saved by recycling one aluminum can.

2. Conserve water and energy, too. Simple tasks like turning off the faucet while you brush your teeth and switching off lights when you leave a room for more than a few minutes will help.

3. Read as much as you can about animals, their habitats and conservation. Share what you've learned with your family, friends and classmates.

4. Visit and support your local zoos.

5. Talk to your teacher about doing a school fund-raising project where the money you raise is sent to a wildlife conservation organization such as your local zoo, the Center for Reproduction of Endangered Species, the World Wildlife Fund or the International Wildlife Federation. Some projects might include a carwash, a bake sale or collecting recycleable items like aluminum cans and newspapers and turning them in for money.

6. Don't buy any products or souvenirs made from exotic animals and discourage everyone you know from doing so. Remember, items like ivory come from animals that have been killed.

7. Write to your congressperson or senator and let him or her know that you feel it's very important to save wildlife.

8. Be creative and try to think of other ways you can help wildlife. The Earth's precious animals are now depending on us for their survival!

BIBLIOGRAPHY

Burt, Olive W. *Rescued! America's Endangered Wildlife on the Comeback Trail.* New York: Julian Messner, 1980.

Day, David. *The Doomsday Book of Animals: A Natural History of Vanished Species.* New York: The Viking Press, 1981.

Hodge, Guy R. *Careers Working With Animals.* Washington, D.C.: Acropolis Books Ltd., 1981.

Nilsson, Greta. *The Endangered Species Handbook.* Washington, D.C.: The Animal Welfare Institute, 1986.

Penny, Malcolm. *The Animal Kingdom: Endangered Animal.* New York: The Bookwright Press, 1988.

Ricciuti, Edward R. *To the Brink of Extinction.* New York, Evanston, San Francisco, London: Harper & Row, Publishers, 1974.

Rinard, Judith E. *Wildlife Making a Comeback.* Washington, D.C.: The National Geographic Society, 1987.

Rinard, Judith E. *Zoos Without Cages.* Washington, D.C.: The National Geographic Society, 1981.

Roth, Charles E. *Then There Were None.* Reading, MA: Addison-Wesley Publishing Company, 1977.

Silverberg, Robert. *The Auk, the Dodo and the Oryx: Vanished and Vanishing Creatures.* New York: Thomas Y. Crowell Company, 1967.

Wexo, John Bonnett. *Endangered Animals: Zoobooks series.* San Diego: Wildlife Education, Ltd., 1983.